IT'S ALL ABOUT

Travel & Vacation

A Leisure Arts Publication by
Nancy M. Hill of

IT'S ALL ABOUT
Travel &
Vacation

ACKNOWLEDGMENTS

It's All About Travel & Vacation is the seventh in a series of books written by NanC and Company and published by Leisure Arts, Inc.

Author: Nancy M. Hill
Design Director: Candice Snyder
Senior Editor: Candice Smoot
Graphic Design: BLT Design
Cover Design: Maren Ogden
Copy Editor: Sharon Staples

Cover Layouts: NanC and Company Design, Susan Stringfellow

For information about sales visit the Leisure Arts web site at www.leisurearts.com

Dear Scrapbooker,

Although this idea book is All About Travel and Vacation, I, personally, like vacationing much more than I do traveling. My favorite place is a quiet, secluded beach where the wind doesn't blow, the sun always shines and cell phones and pagers don't work! But even that, I imagine, could get tiring after a year or two, and I might be interested in rolling over in my lounge chair to look at some of the habitat around me.

They say that half the fun of traveling is the 'anticipation' of going somewhere exciting and the other half may well be the bragging right of having 'been-there-and-done-that!' Whatever the case may be, we have greatly anticipated bringing this fun idea book to press and only wish we had traveled to all the enchanting places that are photographed on these scrapbook pages. We are delighted with the variety of techniques showcased and know that you will find numerous ideas to "scrap-lift" onto your pages.

A new feature in this idea book is our focus on COLOR. We have provided color guidelines and color palette suggestions to enhance your travel scrapbook pages.

Our design staff and submitters continue to amaze us with their creativity and expertise. From world travel to theme parks to camping in the great outdoors, documenting these great times with family and friends will make memories last even longer.

Happy trails to you as you incorporate some of these great techniques and ideas in your travel pages,

Table of Contents

Color

COLOR IS VITAL IN SCRAPBOOKING and can create a mood for your page that is reminiscent of the event you are capturing. Color can stimulate a full range of emotions from happiness to sadness to laughter and tranquility. Good color choice helps create pages that are not only pleasing to the eye, but that promote emotion. Throughout this book you will find color palettes perfect for scrapbooking specific places and themes. Use the colors from the palettes exactly as they are, a variation to meet your needs, or just use the palettes as a guide to what colors go well together.

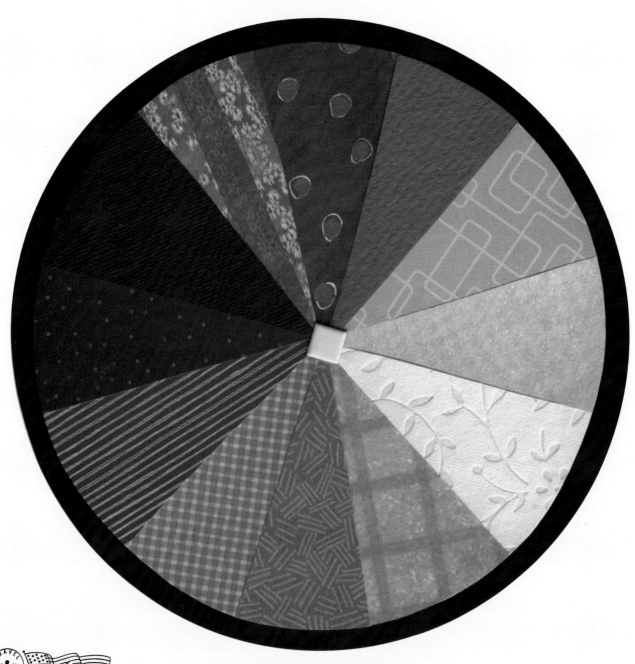

The COLOR WHEEL

The color wheel (see left) is a valuable tool for understanding color, not only does it show the relationship between colors, but it also aids in understanding the following:

Hue: color and hue are equivalent. Red, yellow and blue are primary colors. Orange, green and purple are secondary colors. Tertiary colors are a combination of two secondary colors.

Saturation: the intensity of color. A fully saturated color is considered to be pure; a less saturated, or grayer, color is muted.

Value: the darkness of color. Light colors are referred to as tints, mid-value colors as mid-tones, and dark colors as shades.

Temperature: the warmth or coolness of color. Red, orange and yellow are warm colors recalling fire and the sun. Green, blue and purple are cool colors recalling water and grass.

Monochromatic: a color scheme based on one color. The color variation comes from different saturations and values of that one color.

Analogous: a color scheme based on colors adjacent to each other on the color wheel. These colors work well together because they share the same undertones.

Complimentary: a color scheme based on colors opposite each other on the color wheel. These colors balance and contrast each other, enhancing both colors, making them appear more vibrant.

COLOR AND EMOTIONS

Color evokes emotion. The eye transmits signals to the brain and pituitary gland based on the color it sees creating an emotional reaction. Individuals have unique emotional reactions to color based on their memories, experiences and culture. The following are some common emotional reactions to color:

Red – *exciting, striking, stimulating*
Orange – *energizing, friendly, loud*
Yellow – *sunny, cheerful, warming*
Green – *refreshing, natural, soothing*
Blue – *cool, tranquil, serene, carefree*
Purple – *elegant, valiant, sensual*
Pink – *sweet, youthful, romantic*
Brown – *rustic, rich, earthy, masculine*
Neutrals – *timeless, natural, calming*
White – *pure, innocent, clean, crisp*
Black – *strong, classic, elegant*

All color palettes can be found together on page 63.

Getting There

PACK YOUR BAGS
Page design | Jennifer Parrnelli
Supplies | Cardstock: Bazzill; Patterned Paper: K & Company; Tag: Rebecca Sower; Stickers: All The Extras, Doodlebug Designs Inc., Nostalgiques by EK Success; Rub-ons: Making Memories; Twill Tape: Wrights Ribbon Accent; Acrylic Paint: Plaid Enterprises, Inc.; Labels: Dymo; Font: Two Peas in a Bucket Jack Frost

SEA OF CORTEZ

FUTURE WORLD TRAVELERS
Page design | Sam Cousins
Supplies | Patterned Paper: Sonnets by Creative Imaginations; Fiber: Fibers by the Yard; Brads: Making Memories; Stickers: David Walker; Watch Crystal: Altered Pages; Compass: Altered Pages; Tiles: Us Art Quest; Stamps: PSX Design, Making Memories

MONTEREY

TO BOLDLY GO...
Page design | Ann Gunkel
Supplies | Software: Adobe Photoshop; Font: Weltron Urban

Water & Sand

again we book to the beach for another day. —Thoreau

see Chelle by The SEASHORE

Smelt Sands State Park OREGON COAST Now 2003

SEE CHELLE BY THE SEASHORE
Page design | Jeanne Wynhoff
Supplies | Cardstock: Bazzill; Patterned Paper: Sonnets by Creative Imaginations; Tags: My Mind's Eye, Inc.; Fiber: Fibers by the Yard; Brads: Making Memories; Nail Heads: Jest Charming Embellishments; Stickers: Provo Craft; Mesh: PaperPhernalia; Font: Two Peas in a Bucket Sonnets Script Light

COSTA DEL SOL

BY THE OCEANSIDE
Page design | Martha Crowther
Supplies | Patterned Paper: Wordsworth Stamps; Fibers: Fibers by the Yard; Pewter Shell: Magenta Rubber Stamps; Stickers: Shotz by Creative Imaginations, Wordsworth Stamps; Bamboo Clip: Magic Mesh; Transparency: Hewlett-Packard; Adhesives: Therm O Web, Inc.

The Ocean

The ocean is so very big and I'm so very small,
Isn't it a wonder that God knows us one and all?

The sky is oh so big and blue and seems to never end,
Isn't it a special thing that God gives us good friends?

The sand is soft between my toes and squishy when it's wet,
Isn't it just way too neat that God gave us dogs for pets?

If my mind seems to wander remember that I'm young
And in God's mighty plan for things I've only just begun!

For here I stand so all alone upon God's mighty shore
and even though I'm just a babe he could not love me more!
August 27, 2003   Written by Thena Smith

FROM SEA TO SHINING SEA
Page design | Carrie O'Donnell
Supplies | Cardstock: Bazzill; Vellum: Strathmore Papers;
Page Pebbles: Making Memories; Photo Border: The Print
Shop by Broderbund; Fonts: Dearest Script, Century Gothic

From sea to shining sea.

Pride

Freedom

Peace

PACIFIC SPRAY

ALL ABOARD
Page design | NanC and Company Design
Supplies | Cardstock: DCWV; Patterned Paper: Memories in the Making; Vellum: DCWV; Stamps: Hero Arts Rubber Stamps, Inc

NANTUCKET

COREY LUDINGTON STATE PARK
Page design | Tammy Gauck
Supplies | Patterned Paper: KI Memories; Tag: Avery Dennison; Fiber: Fibers by the Yard; Button: Dress It Up!; Brads: Doodlebug Designs Inc.; Diecut: KI Memories

◄WATER & SAND►

THE LAKE
Page design | Milissa Howes
Supplies | Cardstock: Bazzill; Patterned Paper: NRN Designs; Stickers: Sonnets by Creative Imaginations; Punch: Emagination Crafts, Inc.; Chalk: EK Success

SUMMER CAMP

BEACH BABE
Page design | Tammy Olson
Supplies | Patterned Paper: Provo Craft; Template: Deluxe Designs; Feathers: Zucker Feather Products; Chalk: EK Success; Circle Clip: Making Memories; Beads: Mill Hill

PLAYING IN THE SAND
Page design | Mendy Mitrani
Supplies | Patterned Paper: Memories in
the Making; Stickers: DCWV; Chalk: ColorBox by
Clearsnap, Inc.; Font: Brady Bunch

Max and Noelle have been
friends since kinderGarten
They had a Great time
playing in the sand
at the hill country
hyatt in San Antonio
last summer.
may '03

SAND CASTLE

GULF SHORES
Page design | Lisa Anderson
Supplies | Cardstock: Bazzill; Patterned Paper: NRN Designs; Ribbon Charm: Making Memories; Page Pebble: Leave Memories; Rub-ons: Making Memories; Slide Mount: Leave Memories; Transparency: Magic Scraps

Watch The Wind Blow By

And all I wanna do is let it be and be with you
And watch the wind blow by
And all I wanna see is you and me go on forever
Like the clear blue sky   -Tim McGraw

WATCH THE WIND BLOW BY
Page design | Ginger McSwain
Supplies | Fibers: Scrapgoods; Charm: All The Extras; Font: Van Dijk

SUNRISE TO SUNSET
Page design | NanC and Company Design
Supplies | Cardstock: DCWV; Patterned Paper: Memories in the Making; Fibers: Fibers by the Yard; Page Pebbles: Making Memories

Sunrise to Sunset

Cabo San Lucas Fall '03

MAKING WAVES
Page design | Linda Beeson
Supplies | Cardstock: Making Memories; Patterned Paper: Pebbles, Inc.; Brads: Karen Foster Design; Stickers: Pebbles, Inc., Doodlebug Designs Inc., Wordsworth Stamps

HONEYMOONERS
Page design | Jessica Williams
Supplies | Cardstock: DCWV; Patterned Paper: Memories in the Making; Charms: Memories in the Making

enjoy life

paradise

leave it all behind

refresh

waves

bubbles

ocean

ENJOY LIFE
Page design | NanC and Company Design
Supplies | Cardstock: DCWV; Patterned Paper: Memories in the Making, DCWV; Metal Frame: Making Memories; Metal Hinges: Making Memories; Stickers: SEI; Rub-ons: Making Memories

having a great time

SUMMER FUN
Page design | Tammy Olson
Supplies | Cardstock: Bazzill;
Craft Foam: Darice, Inc.; Stickers:
Provo Craft; Pen: ZIG by EK Success

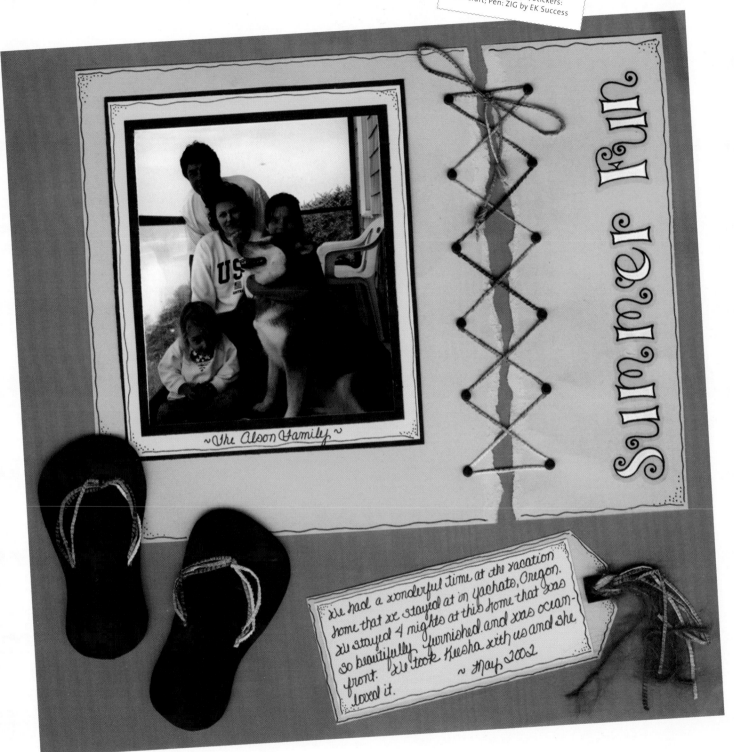

~The Olson Family~

Summer Fun

We had a wonderful time at the vacation home that we stayed at in Yachats, Oregon. We stayed 4 nights at this home that was so beautifully furnished and was ocean-front. We took Keisha with us and she loved it.
~ May 2002

SIESTA TIME
Page design | Sam Cousins
Supplies | Patterned Paper: SEI, Memories in the Making; Stickers: Sonnets by Creative Imaginations, Making Memories, SEI; Watch Crystal: Altered Pages; Walnut Ink: Altered Pages

KYLE
Page design | Becky Dezarn
Supplies | Tag: Making Memories; Metal Quote: Making Memories; Stamp: Making Memories, Stampin' Up; Ink: Close To My Heart, Tsukineko; Embossing Powder: Ranger Industries; Font: Carpenter

FORT WORDEN BEACH
Page design | Tonya Doughty
Supplies | Software: Adobe Photoshop CS

Fort Worden
(Washington)
beach

Our view of June 2003

South of the Border

SAFARI

MOMENTS IN GHANA

Page design | Camille Jensen
Supplies | Cardstock: DCWV; Patterned Paper: DCWV, Memories in the Making; Silver Leaf: Magenta Rubber Stamps; Stickers: Memories in the Making; Mesh: Magenta Rubber Stamps; Stamp: Making Memories

THE GOOD LIFE

Page design | Sam Cousins

Supplies | Patterned Paper: Chatterbox, Inc.; Vellum: Chatterbox, Inc.; Tags: Making Memories; Brads: Making Memories; Stickers: Doodlebug Designs Inc., Creative Imaginations

HAKUNA MATATA
Page design | Linda De Los Reyes
Supplies | Cardstock: Making Memories; Textured Paper: Artistic Scrapper; Conchos: Scrapworks; Shell Charms: Fancifuls, Inc.; Wire: Wild Wire by NSI Innovations; Stamps: Stampin' Up; Embossing Powder: Suze Weinberg; Ink: Versamark by Tsukineko

REMEMBER THIS
Page design | Sam Cousins
Supplies | Patterned Paper: Club Scrap, Inc.; Fibers: Fibers by the Yard; Letters: Foofala; Sticker: Jolee's Boutique, Rebecca Sower; Rub-ons: Making Memories; Stamps: PSX Design

GULF OF GUINEA

Page design | Camille Jensen
Supplies | Cardstock: DCWV;
Patterned Paper: Memories in the
Making; Snaps: Making Memories;
Stickers: Memories in the Making;
Mesh: Magenta Rubber Stamps;
Stamps: Making Memories

◄SOUTH OF THE BORDER►

KASTOM VILLAGE
Page design | Missy Partridge
Supplies | Patterned Paper: Fiskars, Inc.; Textured Paper: Provo Craft; Vellum: The Paper Company; Snaps: Making Memories; Sticker: Nostalgiques by EK Success; Grass Diecuts: Jolee's Boutique; Pen: ZIG by EK Success; Adhesive: ZIG by EK Success; Font: Times New Roman

INDIANA WHO?
Page design | Sam Cousins
Supplies | Cardstock: Club Scrap, Inc.; Fibers: Fibers by the Yard; Brads: Making Memories

HAWAII
Page design | Jessica Williams
Supplies | Cardstock: DCWV; Patterned Paper: Memories in the Making, Provo Craft

VERACRUZ

IT'S NOT A DREAM
Page design | Sue Kelemen
Supplies | Cardstock: Bazzill; Patterned Paper: Two Busy Moms by Deluxe Designs; Fibers: Fibers by the Yard; Metallic Words: DCWV; Brads: Boxer Scrapbooks; Diecuts: QuicKutz; Punch: Emaginations Crafts, Inc.

PARADISE FOUND

Page design | Angela Green
Supplies | Vellum: Stampin' Up;
Diecuts: EK Success; Rub-ons: Making
Memories; Mesh: Magic Mesh; Wax
Seals: Sonnets by Creative Imagina-
tions; Chalk: Stampin' Up; Template:
Deluxe Designs

Park Destinations

England

EPCOT
Walt Disney World

We went to the Rose &
Crown for a bit of a snack.
Perry and I had their
Traditional Sherry Trifle
and the boys had the Rose &
Crown Chocolate Mousse
Parfait. It was lovely.

ENGLAND
Page design | Susan Stringfellow
Supplies | Cardstock: Bazzill; Patterned Paper: Daisy D's Paper
Company; Vellum: Making Memories; Fibers: Fibers by the Yard; Me-
tallic Tags: DCWV; Brads: Making Memories; Maps: Jolee's Boutique;
Photo Corners: Making Memories; Punch: Disney; Stamp: Stampa-
bilities, Stamp Craft; Ink: Stampin' Up; Walnut Ink: Altered Pages;
Transparency: Altered Pages; Fonts: CAC Valiant, Kelly Ann Gothic

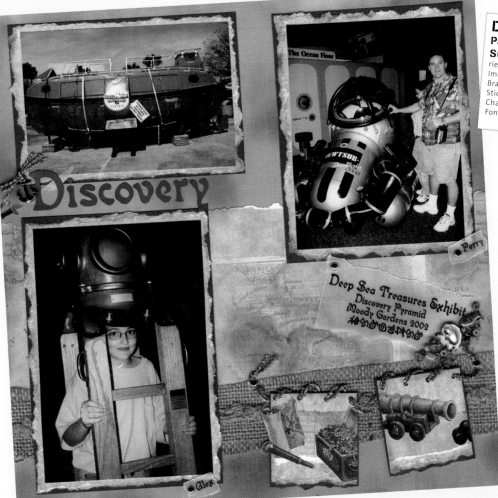

DISCOVERY
Page design | Susan Stringfellow
Supplies | Cardstock: Making Memories; Patterned Paper: Sonnets by Creative Imaginations; Fibers: Fibers by the Yard; Brads: ScrapLovers; Charm: All The Extras; Stickers: NRN Designs; Beads: Crafts Etc.; Chalk: Craft-T Products; Adhesive: JudiKins; Fonts: Atlantix, Atlantean

GUM BALLS

HOGLE ZOO
Page design | Camille Jensen
Supplies | Patterned Paper: Memories in the Making; Textured Paper: Magenta Rubber Stamps; Brads: Lasting Impressions; Floss: DMC; Stamp: Magenta Rubber Stamps, Making Memories, Hero Arts Rubber Stamps, Inc., Wordsworth Stamps

◄PARK DESTINATIONS►

Deutschland

EPCOT

Germany ~ Epcot

We really enjoyed Germany. We did a little shopping, posed with some German Cast Members, and ate dinner at the Biergarten while listening to the Oktoberfest Musikanten.

Germany

Shop for unique gifts, crystal and collectibles here. You'll also find German wines, wine tasting, authentic dining and lederhosen, of course.

DEUTSCHLAND

Page design | Susan Stringfellow

Supplies | Cardstock: Bazzill; Patterned Paper: Memories in the Making; Brads: Making Memories; Paper Clip: Boxer Scrapbooks; Diecut: Memories in the Making; Label Image: Altered Pages; Stickers: Magenta Rubber Stamps; Walnut Ink: Altered Pages; Transparency: 3M Stationary

LEGOLAND

4·22·01

COASTER

LEGOLAND
Page design | Camille Jensen
Supplies | Cardstock: DCWV; Patterned Paper: Memories in the Making; Metallic Frames: DCWV; Overlay: DCWV; Stamps: Making Memories

◄PARK DESTINATIONS►

35

AFRICA
Page design | Susan Stringfellow
Supplies | Cardstock: Bazzill; Patterned Paper: Memories in the Making; Patterned Vellum: EK Success; Fibers: Fibers by the Yard; Buttons: Dress It Up!; Sticker: Altered Pages; Beads: Crafts Etc!; Bamboo Clips: Altered Pages; Trim: Altered Pages; Mesh: ScrapLovers; Chalk: ColorBox by Clearsnap, Inc.; Stamps: Dollar Tree; Ink: Tsukineko; Transparency: Altered Pages; Font: African

SPLASH MOUNTAIN
Page design | Susan Stringfellow
Supplies | Cardstock: Bazzill; Patterned Paper: Memories in the Making; Fibers: Fibers by the Yard; Diecut: Memories in the Making; Chalk: ColorBox by Clearsnap, Inc.; Stamps: Making Memories; Ink: Stampin' Up; Transparency: 3M Stationary; Adhesive: JudiKins; Font: Antique Type

Entrance →

SPLASH MOUNTAIN

Cooling off and Splashing Down!!!

july '02 W.D.W.

Zip-a-dee-doo-dah
Zip-adee-ay
My oh my what a
wonderful day
Plenty of sunshine
headed our way
Zip-a-dee-doo-dah
Zip-a-dee-ay

Mr. Blue Bird on my
shoulder
It's the truth, it's actual
Everything is satisfactual
Zip-a-dee-doo-dah
Zip-a-dee-ay
Wonderful feeling,
wonderful Day!

briar patch!

The Great Outdoors

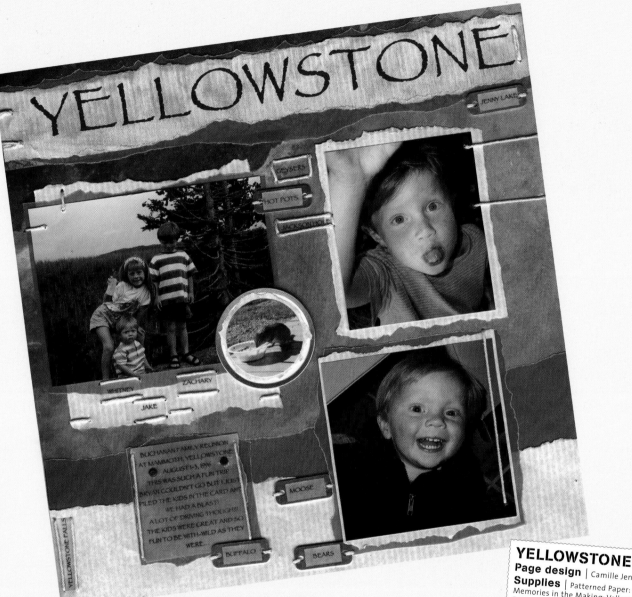

YELLOWSTONE
Page design | Camille Jensen
Supplies | Patterned Paper:
Memories in the Making; Vellum:
DCWV; Tags: Darice, Inc.; Metal Em-
bellishments: Making Memories

MORNING GLORY

THE SNAKE

Page design | NanC and Company Design
Supplies | Cardstock: DCWV; Patterned
Paper: Memories in the Making; Metallic Frame:
DCWV

A SCENE
OF BEAUTY

Page design | NanC and Company Design
Supplies | Cardstock: DCWV; Patterned
Paper: Memories in the Making; Brads: Making
Memories; Stickers: Memories in the Making,
Making Memories

A scene of beauty

Smoky

Camping Vacation 2002

Mountains

Gatlinburg, Tennesse

beauty
peace
quiet
fun
nature
park
dollywood
smiles

SMOKY MOUNTAIN RAFTING
Page design | Tracey Clark
Supplies | Patterned Paper: Chatterbox, Inc.; Diecut: QuicKutz

Our Camping Trip

OUR CAMPING TRIP
Page design | Jessica Williams
Supplies | Cardstock: DCWV; Metallic Frame: DCWV; Metallic Word: DCWV; Metallic Letters: DCWV

f i s h i n g

LODGEPOLE PINE

DAN
Page design | NanC and Company Design
Supplies | Cardstock: DCWV; Metal Frame:
Making Memories; Metal Clip: Making Memories;
Brads: Making Memories; Page Pebbles: Making
Memories; Vellum Quote: DCWV; Sticker: Paper Bliss
by Westrim Crafts

The best and most beautiful things in the world cannot be seen or even touched... They must be felt with the heart.

–Helen Keller

d a n

Nature's Inspirations

TREE OF LIFE
Page design | Lisa Anderson
Supplies | Cardstock: Bazzill; Patterned Paper: Hot Off The Press; Tag: Avery Dennison; Page Pebble: Making Memories; Beads: Blue Moon Beads; Stamp: Inkadinkado; Ink: Versamark by Tsukineko; Embossing Powder: Stamps 'n' Stuff

TULIPS

MOSS GARDEN

Perhaps this is just another ORDINARY TREE...
But take another look –
    Do you see the *arrow* at the tree base?

Now can you fathom the tree's
    ENORMOUS SIZE??

ORDINARY TREE
Page design | Briana Fisher
Supplies | Cardstock : DCWV

FIRST FROST
Page design | NanC and Company Design
Supplies | Cardstock: DCWV; Patterned Paper:
Memories in the Making; Tag: Making Memories;
Metallic Frame: DCWV; Metallic Letters: DCWV

**WATERFALLS
OF WONDER**
Page design | NanC and Company Design
Supplies | Cardstock: DCWV; Patterned
Paper: Memories in the Making; Floss: Making
Memories; Ribbon: Offray & Son, Inc.

◄NATURE'S INSPIRATIONS►

Sight Seeing

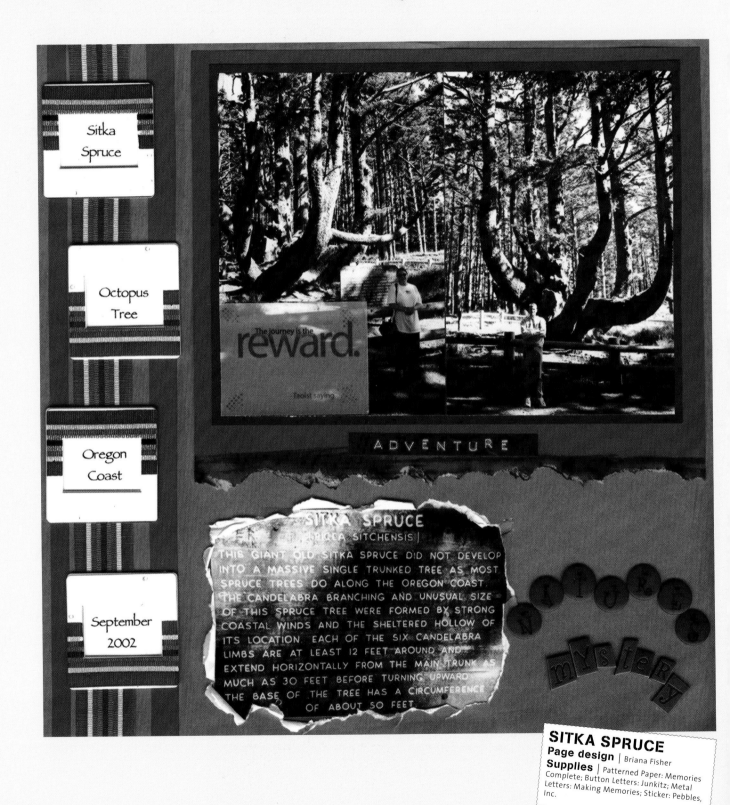

Sitka
Spruce

Octopus
Tree

Oregon
Coast

September
2002

The journey is the
reward.

Taoist saying

ADVENTURE

SITKA SPRUCE
| PICEA SITCHENSIS |
THIS GIANT OLD SITKA SPRUCE DID NOT DEVELOP
INTO A MASSIVE SINGLE TRUNKED TREE AS MOST
SPRUCE TREES DO ALONG THE OREGON COAST.
THE CANDELABRA BRANCHING AND UNUSUAL SIZE
OF THIS SPRUCE TREE WERE FORMED BY STRONG
COASTAL WINDS AND THE SHELTERED HOLLOW OF
ITS LOCATION. EACH OF THE SIX CANDELABRA
LIMBS ARE AT LEAST 12 FEET AROUND AND
EXTEND HORIZONTALLY FROM THE MAIN TRUNK AS
MUCH AS 30 FEET BEFORE TURNING UPWARD.
THE BASE OF THE TREE HAS A CIRCUMFERENCE
OF ABOUT 50 FEET

NATURE
mystery

SITKA SPRUCE
Page design | Briana Fisher
Supplies | Patterned Paper: Memories
Complete; Button Letters: Junkitz; Metal
Letters: Making Memories; Sticker: Pebbles,
Inc.

DUSK

DEEP WEST
Page design | Catherine Lucas
Supplies | Cardstock: The Rusty Pickle; Tag: Making Memories; Fiber: Fibers by the Yard; Eyelets: Making Memories

WYOMING
Page design | Catherine Lucas
Supplies | Cardstock: The Rusty Pickle; Stickers: Karen Foster Design; Slide Frame: Club Scrap, Inc.; Font: Textile

where in the
WORLD...

be an explorer
the universe is filled with
wonder and magical things

—flavia

WHERE IN THE WORLD
Page design | Christine Johnson
Supplies | Cardstock: Bazzill; Patterned Paper: Anna Griffin, Mustard
Moon Paper Co.; Rub-ons: Making Memories; Font: Two Peas in a Bucket
Falling Leaves

FREEDOM
Page design | Pam Rawn

Supplies | Tag: Making Memories; Dog Tag: Li'l Davis Designs; Flag Tag: The Paper Loft; Metal Words: Making Memories; Metal Mesh: Making Memories; Screw Eyelets: Making Memories; Rub-ons: Making Memories; Ribbon: Making Memories; Photo Clips: Making Memories; Twistel: Making Memories; Bookplate: Li'l Davis Designs; Safety Pins: Li'l Davis Designs; Mesh: Magic Scraps; Stamp: Hero Arts Rubber Stamps, Inc.; Ink: Versamark by Tsukineko, Stampin' Up; Font: Daniel

MOJAVE

FARMERS MARKET
Page design | Susan Stringfellow

Supplies | Patterned Paper: Memories Complete; Button Letters: Cardstock: Making Memories; Patterned Paper: Memories in the Making; Fibers: Fibers by the Yard; Thread: Coats & Clark; Brads: Making Memories; Stickers: Memories in the Making; Rivet: Chatterbox, Inc.; Ink: Stampin' Up; Walnut Ink: Altered Pages; Embossing Powder: Stamps 'n' Stuff; Labels: Altered Pages; Transparency: 3M Stationary; Foam Tape: Magic Mounts

NINA

Page design | Carla Jacobsen

Supplies | Patterned Paper: Colorbok, Hot Off The Press; Fibers: Adornments by EK Success; Eyelets: Making Memories; Snaps: Making Memories; Stickers: Sonnets by Creative Imaginations; Rub-ons: Craf-T Products; Chalk: EK Success

AMISH COUNTRY

Page design | NanC and Company Design

Supplies | Cardstock: DCWV; Patterned Paper: Memories in the Making; Metallic Frame: DCWV; Brads: Making Memories; Slide Mount: Magic Scraps; Floss: Making Memories

MIDGET MAN MARCH
Page design | Ann Gunkel
Supplies | Software: Adobe Photoshop; Font: Weltron Urban

NEW YORK
Page design | Jessica Williams
Supplies | Cardstock: DCWV; Patterned Paper: Memories in the Making; Sticker: Memories in the Making

Foreign Lands

JAPAN
Page design | Camille Jensen
Supplies | Cardstock: DCWV; Metallic Tags: DCWV; Photo Overlay: DCWV; Charms: Memories in the Making

LONDON
Page design | Camille Jensen
Supplies | Cardstock: DCWV; Patterned Paper: Memories in the Making; Metallic Frame: DCWV; Metallic Tag: DCWV; Stickers: Pebbles, Inc.; Page Pebbles: Making Memories; Slide Mount: Magic Scraps; Acrylic Paints: Making Memories; Stamps: Making Memories, Hero Arts Rubber Stamps, Inc.

STAINED GLASS

TOWER OF LONDON
Page design | Camille Jensen
Supplies | Cardstock: DCWV; Patterned Paper: Memories in the Making; Metallic Frame: DCWV; Metallic Tag: DCWV; Stickers: Pebbles, Inc.; Page Pebbles: Making Memories; Slide Mount: Magic Scraps; Acrylic Paints: Making Memories; Stamps: Making Memories, Hero Arts Rubber Stamps, Inc.

THE SANDS &
SAILS OF FRANCE
Page design | NanC and Company Design
Supplies | Cardstock: DCWV; Patterned Paper:
Memories in the Making; Metal Frames: Making
Memories, DCWV; Stickers: Memories in the Making;
Page Pebble: Making Memories

the SANDS SAILS of France

THE EMPEROR'S
SUMMER PALACE
Page design | NanC and Company Design
Supplies | Cardstock: DCWV; Patterned
Paper: Memories in the Making; Metal Frame:
DCWV; Photo Corners: Memories in the Making;
Tiles: EK Success

Fall 1999
China

the
Emperor's Summer
Palace

was a magnificent sight. Even though
it was not very far from the Forbidden
City, it must have felt nice to be able
to escape to the river bank. The architecture
was magnificent & we enjoyed the day exploring.

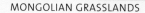

MONGOLIAN GRASSLANDS

TRAVEL TAG
Design | Tammy Gauck
Supplies | Patterned Paper:
7 Gypsies; Fibers: Fibers by the
Yard; Buttons: Dress It Up!; Stamp:
Stampin' Up

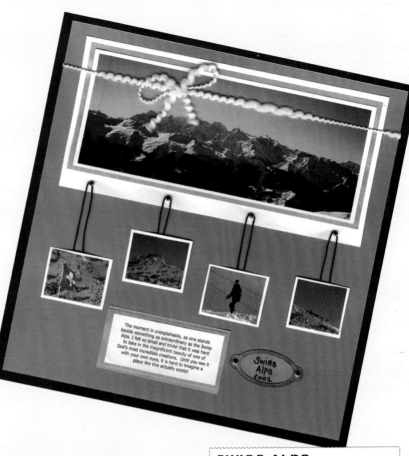

SWISS ALPS
Page design | NanC and Company Design
Supplies | Cardstock: DCWV; Patterned
Paper: Memories in the Making; Metal Frame:
DCWV; Brads: Making Memories

ANDALUSIA

LAVENDER FIELDS

THE STREETS OF FRANCE BY FOOT

Page design | NanC and Company Design
Supplies | Cardstock: DCWV; Patterned Paper: Memories in the Making; Stickers: Nostalgiques by EK Success

memories

EUROPEAN GETAWAY
Page design | NanC and Company Design
Supplies | Cardstock: DCWV; Patterned Paper:
Memories in the Making; Tag: DCWV; Metal Letters:
Making Memories; Button: DCWV

These scenes of the French Riviera were taken on our trip to France in 1998. The water makes a beautiful background for the city.

vacation

remember

ROME IN RUINS
Page design | Camille Jensen
Supplies | Cardstock: DCWV; Patterned Paper: Memories in the Making; Stamps: Making Memories

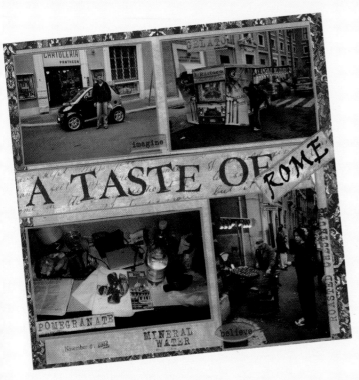

VINCENT

FRESH FLOWERS OF FRANCE
Page design | NanC and Company Design
Supplies | Cardstock: DCWV; Patterned Paper:
Memories in the Making; Metal Hinge: Making
Memories

Fresh
Flowers
of
France

PEN PALS
Page design | Misty Posey
Supplies | Cardstock: Bazzill; Vellum: Paper Garden; Fibers: Fibers by the Yard; Mesh: Jest Charming Embellishments, Magic Scraps; Slide Mount: All The Extras; Stamps: A Stamp in the Hand Co.; Ink: Rubber Stampede; Embossing Powder: Stamps 'n' Stuff; Font: Two Peas in a Bucket Stained Glass

There is nothing on this earth to be more prized than...True Friendship

An Afternoon at the Chinese Market

One of my mom's favorite things to do in a foreign country is to go to the market. She loves to see how other people shop and what foods are available. This market was very unique, lining the streets in Beijing. They sold everything from baked goods and spices to fresh meat and produce. It was an enjoyable experience except when getting a whiff of the fish!

CHINESE MARKET
Page design | NanC and Company Design
Supplies | Cardstock: DCWV; Patterned Vellum: Memories in the Making; Button: Making Memories

SUNRISE 'TIL SUNSET

Page design | NanC and Company Design
Supplies | Cardstock: DCWV; Patterned Paper: Memories in the Making; Tags: Making Memories; Rub-ons: Making Memories; Floss: Making Memories; Charm: Making Memories; Ribbon: Offray & Son, Inc.

Our trip to France

SUNRISE til SUNSET

TRAVEL TAG

Page design | Tammy Gauck
Supplies | Patterned Paper: Mustard Moon Paper Co., 7 Gypsies; Fibers: Fibers by the Yard; Stamps: Stampington & Company, Stampin' Up

Journey

Coming Home

Almost Home...

love

ALMOST HOME
Page design | Thena Smith
Supplies | Software: Digital Image Pro; Background Papers: Cottage Arts; Mats: Cottage Arts; Embellishments: Cottage Arts

BIG SPRINGS

THE END
Page design | Sam Cousins
Supplies | Patterned Paper: 7 Gypsies, DCWV; Fibers: Fibers by the Yard; Brad: Making Memories; Stickers: All My Memories, Wordsworth Stamps; Money Embellishments: Jolee's Boutique

The End!

You are probably thinking that this is an old way to end our vacation scrapbook. After all, it is a photo of Po counting his money. Well, this is the way ALL of our vacations have ALWAYS ended. From the very moment that our vacations begin, we are given a lecture on the importance of keeping every receipt. We can always tell when our vacation is nearing the end. Po pulls out the receipts, his calculator and his cross pen. Then all of the money gets divided into piles. Appropriate currency conversions are made. And the fun begins. The quest..."HOW MUCH DID THIS VACATION COST ME???" We never hear the totals, just the phrase "way too much!". But the fun doesn't end there. When we get back on the plane to come home, out come the receipts, the calculator and the cross pens again. Just to do a double check and to have our custom forms

"He's an accountant...he can't help it!"

Stas visted the Carousel in Bryant Park. This lovely mid-town park has an old-fashioned carousel that Stasiu loves! He even rode it twice--once on the Rabbit with Mommy & once on the Frog with Daddy!

Nothing is more fun than FOOD in New York. Uncle Paulie joined us for a super dinner at Chef Mario Batali's Lupa. Two hours later, Stas was still a great boy--loving the boutique prosciutto, eating gnocchi alla romana and inhaling chocolate tartuffo gelato for dessert!

NEW YORK
Page design | Ann Gunkel
Supplies | Software: Adobe Photoshop;

To commemorate our spectacular Autumn in New York, I wrote a book, starring our son, Stas. Designed in glossy magazine style, the book traces our steps, highlighting the sights, sounds & tastes of New York. The book was then laminated and bound for my son's Christmas present. We love reading it and reliving the fun again & again. Its the best vacation souvenier I can think of!

ALOHA

◄COMING HOME►

Sources

3M Stationary
(800) 364-3577
3m.com

A Stamp in the Hand Co.
(310) 884-9700
astampinthehand.com

Adobe
(800) 833-6687
adobe.com

All My Memories
(888) 553-1998
allmymemories.com

All The Extras
(425) 868-6628
alltheextras.com

Altered Pages
alteredpages.com

Anna Griffin
(888) 817-8170
annagriffin.com

Artistic Scrapper
(818) 786-8304
artisticscrapper.com

Avery Dennison
averydennison.com

Bazzill
(480) 558-8557
bazzillbasics.com

Blue Moon Beads
(800) 377-6715
beads.net

Boxer Scrapbooks
(888) 625-6255
boxerscrapbooks.com

Broderbund
(415) 382-4400
broderbund.com

Chatterbox, Inc.
(888) 416-6260
chatterboxinc.com

Clearsnap, Inc.
(800) 448-4862
clearsnap.com

Close To My Heart
(888) 655-6552
closetomyheart.com

Club Scrap, Inc.
(888) 634-9100
clubscrap.com

Coats & Clark
coatsandclark.com

Colorbok
(800) 366-4660
colorbok.com

Cottage Arts
cottagearts.net

Craf-T Products
(800) 530-3410
craf-tproducts.com

Crafts Etc!
(800) 888-0321
craftsetc.com

Creative Imaginations
(800) 942-6487
cigift.com

Daisy D's Paper Company
(888) 601-8955
daisydspaper.com

Darice, Inc.
(800) 321-1494
darice.com

DCWV
(801) 224-6766
diecutswithaview.com

Deluxe Designs
(480) 497-9005
deluxecuts.com

Disney
go.disney.com

DMC
(973) 589-9890
dmc-usa.com

Dollar Tree
757-321-5000
dollartree.com

Doodlebug Designs Inc.
801-966-9952
timelessmemories.ca

Dress It Up!
dressitup.com

Dymo
dymo.com

EK Success
(800) 524-1349
eksuccess.com

Emagination Crafts, Inc.
(630) 833-9521
emaginationcrafts.com

Fancifuls, Inc.
(607) 849-6870
fancifulsinc.com

Fibers by the Yard
fibersbytheyard.com

Fiskars, Inc.
(715) 842-2091
fiskars.com

Foofala
(402) 758-0863
foofala.com

Hero Arts Rubber Stamps, Inc.
(800) 822-4376
heroarts.com

Hewlett-Packard
hp.com

Hot Off The Press
(800) 227-9595
paperpizazz.com

Inkadinkado
(781) 938-6100
inkadinkado.com

Jest Charming Embellishments
(702) 564-5101
jestcharming.com

Jolee's Boutique
joleesbyyou.com

JudiKins
(310) 515-1115
judikins.com

Junkitz
junkitz.com

K & Company
(888) 244-2083
kandcompany.com

Karen Foster Design
(801) 451-9779
karenfosterdesign.com

KI Memories
kimemories.com

Leave Memories
leavememories.com

Li'l Davis Designs
(949) 838-0344
lildavisdesigns.com

Magenta Rubber Stamps
magentarubberstamps.com

Magic Mesh
magicmesh.com

Magic Mounts
(800) 332-0050
magicmounts.com

Magic Scraps
(972) 238-1838
magicscraps.com

Making Memories
(800) 286-5263
makingmemories.com

Memories Complete
(866) 966-6365
memoriescomplete.com

Memories in the Making
(800) 643-8030
leisurearts.com

Mill Hill
millhill.com

Mustard Moon Paper Co.
(408) 229-8542
mustardmoon.com

My Mind's Eye, Inc.
(801) 298-3709
frame-ups.com

NRN Designs
nrndesigns.com

NSI Innovations
nsiinnovations.com

Paper Company, The
(800) 426-8989
thepaperco.com

Paper Garden
(210) 494-9602
papergarden.com

PaperPhernalia
paperphernalia.com

Pebbles, Inc.
pebblesinc.com

Plaid Enterprises, Inc.
(800) 842-4197
plaidonline.com

Provo Craft
(888) 577-3545
provocraft.com

PSX Design
(800) 782-6748
psxdesign.com

QuicKutz
(888) 702-1146
quickutz.com

Ranger Industries
(800) 244-2211
rangerink.com

Rebecca Sower
mississippipaperarts.com

Rubber Stampede
(800) 423-4135
rubberstampede.com

Rusty Pickle, The
(801) 274-9588
rustypickle.com

Scrapgoods
scrapgoods.com

ScrapLovers
scraplovers.com

Scrapworks
scrapworksllc.com

SEI
(800) 333-3279
shopsei.com

Stamp Craft
stampcraft.com.au

Stampabilities
stampabilities.com

Stampin' Up
(800) 782-6787
stampinup.com

Stampington & Company
(949) 380-7318

Stamps 'n' Stuff
(515) 331-4307
stampsnstuff.com

Strathmore Papers
(800) 628-8816
strathmore.com

Suze Weinberg
(732) 761-2400
schmoozewithsuze.com

Therm O Web, Inc.
(800) 323-0799
thermoweb.com

Tsukineko
(800) 769-6633
tsukineko.com

Two Peas in a Bucket
twopeasinabucket.com

Us Art Quest
(517) 522-6225
usartquest.com

Westrim Crafts
(800) 727-2727
westrimcrafts.com

Wordsworth Stamps
(719) 282-3495
wordsworthstamps.com

Wrights Ribbon Accents
(877) 597-4448

Zucker Feather Products
(573) 796-2183
zuckerfeathers.com

COLOR PALETTES

GETTING THERE

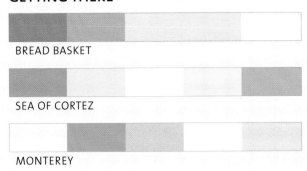

BREAD BASKET

SEA OF CORTEZ

MONTEREY

WATER & SAND

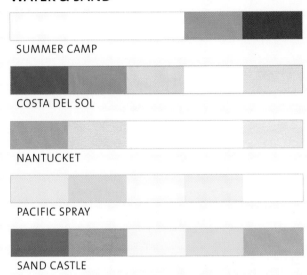

SUMMER CAMP

COSTA DEL SOL

NANTUCKET

PACIFIC SPRAY

SAND CASTLE

SOUTH OF THE BORDER

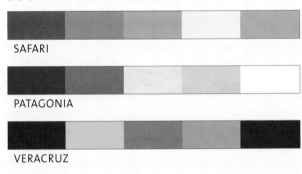

SAFARI

PATAGONIA

VERACRUZ

PARK DESTINATIONS

GUM BALLS

COASTER

THE GREAT OUTDOORS

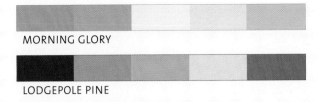

MORNING GLORY

LODGEPOLE PINE

NATURE'S INSPIRATIONS

TULIPS

MOSS GARDEN

SIGHT SEEING

DUSK

MOJAVE

FOREIGN LANDS

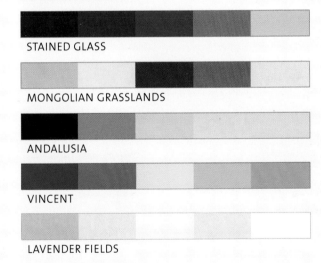

STAINED GLASS

MONGOLIAN GRASSLANDS

ANDALUSIA

VINCENT

LAVENDER FIELDS

COMING HOME

ALOHA

BIG SPRINGS

Look for these published or soon to be published Leisure Arts Scrapbooking Idea Books

IT'S ALL IN YOUR IMAGINATION

IT'S ALL ABOUT BABY

IT'S ALL ABOUT SCHOOL

IT'S ALL ABOUT TECHNIQUE

IT'S ALL ABOUT CARDS AND TAGS

IT'S ALL ABOUT MINI ALBUMS

IT'S ALL ABOUT TRAVEL AND VACATION

IT'S ALL ABOUT PETS AND ANIMALS

IT'S ALL ABOUT HERITAGE PAGES

IT'S ALL ABOUT TEENS

10-20-30 MINUTE SCRAPBOOK PAGES